# THE
# DAFFODIL PRINCIPLE

story by JAROLDEEN ASPLUND EDWARDS

illustrations by ANNE MARIE OBORN

one woman • two hands • one bulb at a time

SHADOW
MOUNTAIN

*Photography support by Cynthia Dye*

Text © 2004 Jaroldeen Asplund Edwards

Illustrations © 2004 Anne Marie Oborn

Visit us at shadowmountain.com

**Library of Congress Cataloging-in-Publication Data**

Edwards, Jaroldeen.
  The daffodil principle / text by Jaroldeen Asplund Edwards ; illustrations by Anne Marie Oborn.
    p.    cm.
  ISBN 1-59038-224-2 (alk. paper)
  1. Self-actualization (Psychology)    2. Success—Psychological aspects.    I. Title.
BF637.S4 E4 2004
158.1—dc22

2003023984

Printed in Shenzhen, China
R. R. Donnelley and Sons

18961-7170

10   9   8   7   6   5   4   3   2   1

I wandered lonely as a cloud

That floats on high o'er vales and hills,

When all at once I saw a crowd,

A host, of golden daffodils.

WILLIAM WORDSWORTH, 1770–1850

Twice my daughter Carolyn had phoned to say, "Mother, you must come see the daffodils before they are over."

I wanted to go, but it was a two-hour drive from Laguna to Lake Arrowhead. Going and coming would take most of a day—and I honestly did not have a free day until the following week.

"I'll come next Tuesday," I promised, a little reluctantly, on her third call.

Tuesday dawned cold and rainy. Still, I had promised, and so I determinedly drove the length of Route 91, continued on I-215, and finally turned onto Route 18 to drive up the mountain. The summit was swathed in clouds, and I had gone only a few miles when a wet, gray blanket of fog covered the highway. I slowed to a crawl, my heart pounding.

The road became narrow and winding toward the top of the mountain. I executed each hazardous turn at a snail's pace. I was praying to reach the turnoff at Blue Jay that would signify I had arrived at my daughter's street.

When I finally walked into Carolyn's house and hugged and greeted my grand-children, I said, "Forget the daffodils, Carolyn! The road is invisible in clouds and fog, and there is nothing in the world except you and these darling children that I want to see enough to drive another inch!"

My daughter smiled calmly. "We drive in this all the time, Mother."

"Well, you won't get *me* back on the road until it clears—and then I'm heading for home!" I assured her.

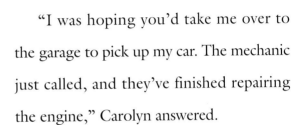

"I was hoping you'd take me over to the garage to pick up my car. The mechanic just called, and they've finished repairing the engine," Carolyn answered.

"How far will we have to drive?" I asked cautiously.

"Just a few blocks," she said cheerfully. So we bundled up the children and went out to my car. "I'll drive," Carolyn offered. "I'm used to this weather."

We got into the car, and my daughter began driving. In a few minutes I was aware that we were back on the Rim-of-the-World road, heading over the top of the mountain.

"Where are we going?" I exclaimed, distressed to be back on the mountain road in the fog. "This isn't the way to the garage!"

"We're going to the garage the long way," Carolyn smiled, "by way of the daffodils."

"Carolyn," I said sternly, trying to sound as if I were still the mother and in control of the situation, "please turn around. There is nothing in the world worth driving on this road in this weather."

"It's all right, Mother," she replied with a knowing grin. "I know what I'm doing. I promise. You will never forgive yourself if you miss this experience."

And so my sweet, darling daughter, who had never given me a minute of difficulty in her whole life, was suddenly in charge— and she was kidnapping me! I couldn't believe it. Like it or not, I was on the way to see some ridiculous daffodils—driving through the thick, gray silence of the mist-wrapped mountaintop at what I thought was risk to life and limb. I muttered all the way.

After about twenty minutes we turned onto a small gravel road that branched down into an oak-filled hollow on the side of the mountain. The fog had lifted a bit, but the sky was lowering, gray and heavy with clouds. We parked in a small parking lot adjacent to a little stone church. From our vantage point we could see, beyond us in the mist, the crests of the San Bernardino range like the dark, humped backs of a herd of elephants. Far below us the fog-shrouded valleys, hills, and flatlands stretched away to the desert.

On the far side of the church I saw a path covered in pine needles. Before us there were towering evergreens, riotous manzanita bushes, and an inconspicuous, hand-lettered sign, "Daffodil Garden."

We each took a child's hand, and I followed Carolyn down the path as it wound through the silent, giant trees. The mountain sloped away in irregular dips, folds, and valleys, like a deeply creased skirt. Live oaks, mountain laurel, shrubs, and bushes clustered in the folds, and in the gray, drizzling air, the green foliage looked dark and monochromatic. I shivered. Then we turned a sharp corner along the path, and I gasped.

Before me lay the most glorious sight! Unexpected and completely splendid. It looked as if someone had taken the great gold vat of the sun and poured it over the mountain peak and slopes, where it had run over every rise and into every crevice. Even in the mist-filled air, the mountainside was radiant with light, clothed in massive drifts and waves of daffodils. The flowers grew in majestic swirls, great ribbons and swaths of deep orange, soft white, lemon yellow, salmon pink, rich saffron, and butter yellow. Each different-colored variety (I learned later that there were more than thirty-five varieties of daffodils in the vast display) was planted as a group so that it swelled and flowed like its own river with its own unique hue.

In the center of this dazzling display, a cascade of purple grape hyacinths poured down the slope like a waterfall of blossoms framed in its own rock-lined basin.

A charming path wound through the garden. There were several resting places, paved with stone and furnished with Victorian wooden benches and great tubs of coral and carmine tulips.

As if this were not magnificence enough, Mother Nature added her own grace notes. Above the daffodils, a bevy of western bluebirds flitted and darted, flashing their brilliance. These charming little birds, sapphire blue with breasts of magenta red, danced in the air, their colors sparkling like jewels. Above the blowing, glowing daffodils, the effect was breathtaking.

It did not matter that the sun was not shining. The radiance of the daffodils was like the glow of the brightest sunlit day. Words, wonderful as they are, simply cannot describe the incredible beauty of that flower-bedecked mountaintop.

Five acres of flowers! (This too I discovered later.) "But who has done this?" I asked Carolyn. I was overflowing with gratitude that she had brought me here—even against my will. This was a once-in-a-lifetime experience. "Who?" I asked again, almost speechless with wonder, "and how, and why, and when?"

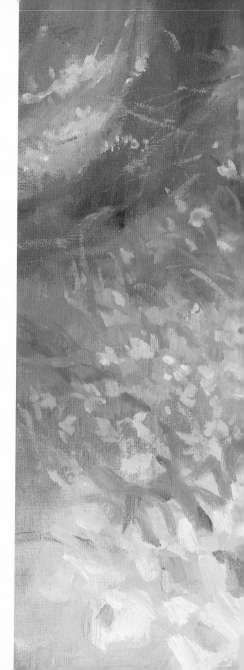

"It's just one woman," Carolyn answered. "That's her home." My daughter pointed to a well-kept A-frame house that looked small and modest in the midst of all that glory.

We walked up to the house, my mind buzzing with questions. On the patio we saw a poster with the headline, "Answers to the Questions I Know You Are Asking." The first answer was a simple one: "50,000 bulbs," it read. The second answer was, "One at a time. One woman. Two hands, two feet, and very little brain." The third answer was, "Began in 1958."

There it was. The Daffodil Principle. For me that moment was a life-changing experience. I thought of this woman who, decades before, had begun—one bulb at a time—to bring her vision of beauty and joy to an obscure mountaintop.

One bulb at a time. There was no other way to do it. One bulb at a time. No shortcuts—simply loving the slow process of planting. Loving the work as it unfolded. Loving an achievement that grew slowly and bloomed for only three weeks of each year.

Still, by planting one small bulb at a time, year after year, this quiet woman had forever changed the world in which she lived.

I mused aloud. "What could I have accomplished had I approached some inspired project as this woman did?"

My wise daughter glanced at me with a smile. "Don't be discouraged. Start today."

She was right. We can choose a goal and begin to move toward it. By multiplying tiny pieces of time with increments of daily effort, we can accomplish magnificent things. We, too, can change our world.